RUPTURE

Praise for Susan Varga

The directness and simplicity of these poems, beautifully arranged as stages in a recovery, carry the urgency, honesty and celebration of a life reclaimed.

JOAN LONDON

Susan Varga writes that until recently she thought of herself as a prose writer. Her first collection of poetry suggests that the poet she very clearly is was forming quietly but determinedly over a lifetime. The poems that comprise Rupture are lucid, deft, unapologetic, forthright. There are images and lines that are literally breath-taking, stanzas that punch with wisdom, and whole poems that linger long after the book is finished. The rupture of the title was caused by a severe stroke experienced by the writer and her subsequent remaking and embrace of a changed life. The stroke poems form part of this collection, but as well there are poems that draw on nature, ageing, friendship, home and enduring love, all laid bare with an insight and lyricism that makes Rupture a rewarding and powerful collection.

ANDREA GOLDSMITH

About the Author

Susan Varga has worked in film and video and briefly as a lawyer. Her first book, *Heddy and Me* won the Christina Stead Award for non-fiction. It was followed by the award-winning novel *Happy Families*, then *Broometime* (2001), co-authored by Anne Coombs. Her most recent novel was *Headlong* (UWAP, 2009), which was short-listed for the Barbara Jefferis Award. *Rupture* is her first book of poetry.

RUPTURE

POEMS (2012–2015)

BY

SUSAN

VARGA

UWA PUBLISHING

First published in 2016 by
UWA Publishing
Crawley, Western Australia 6009
www.uwap.uwa.edu.au

UWAP is an imprint of UWA Publishing
a division of The University of Western Australia

THE UNIVERSITY OF
WESTERN
AUSTRALIA

National Library of Australia
Cataloguing-in-Publication entry:

Varga, Susan, author.
Rupture / Susan Varga.
ISBN: 9781742589091 (paperback)
Australian poetry.
Cerebrovascular disease—Poetry.
Diseases—Poetry.
A821.3

Typeset in Bembo by Lasertype
Cover image from an original painting from Dale Dean
Printed by Lightning Source

This project has been assisted by the Australian Government through the
Australia Council, its arts funding and advisory body.

Australian Government

Australia
Council
for the Arts

uwapublishing

Contents

III NIGHT

IV ALONE IN THE CITY

V BRUNSWICK HEADS

I

MASTERSTROKE

Spaceship

The room floats on humming air.
The nurse's station suspended
in a greenish light,
beams invisible signals.
Our beds gently circle it,
as if tethered.
Benign murmuring of machines.
Far away sounds of the street below.

Spaceship ICU.
Bathed in green amniotic fluid,
sandpaper mouth, swelling tongue,
body afloat
in another dimension.
Never have I felt so safe.

Different Strokes

1.

A stroke of luck.
Someone was there
to help.

Where are my legs?

In Emergency they stroke
my right arm –
a prickly thing.

Not mine.

Where are words?
If they are gone for good
who am I?

2.

In the Stroke Unit they feed
me pap in case I choke.
They prod me for words.
Name, day, month, year.

Wedged between flowers
and euphoria I laugh often,
an unfamiliar gurgling laugh.
I watch light fall on a picture

In Rehab, mostly stroke patients.
They prod our dangling
strangers' limbs.
'Ten times! Twenty times!'

After four weeks
they take the wheelchair away
and give me a stick.

3.

Winter now. Other hospital
closer to home.
Bare branches, cold air.
Long linoleum corridors
all shiny.
A room of my own!

I stroke weakly through
tepid water in the Rehab pool.
My dead mother swam
a strong smooth stroke.
Will she help me
on this journey back?

4.

On weekend leave
I stroke the dogs.
My right hand can't
feel their fine fur.
But they lean against me
as of old.

Back in hospital I write
this for the therapist:

'Home!!
Dogs – Sasah, Boidie, Gi—gr
See new house – galde
Luche
A day big'

The Ward Quartet

The Bed Opposite

She enters the ward,
hair dressed, make-up perfected,
china-blues eyes.
Pretty as a picture –
she's always known it.

She changes into a quilted
china-blue dressing gown.
Jaunty, refreshing her lipstick.
'I've had three little stokes,
y'know'.

The boyfriend, pushing eighty,
is old school. A war hero.
Late love.
They hold hands, talk of modifying
stairs and kitchen
for when she comes home.

In the bleak dining room
she holds court, blonded hair,
blue dressing-gown refulgent
among the broken-down blokes
waiting for the midday meal.

One morning she starts
to ramble, jumbles her words.

Her legs won't walk her
to the dining room
anymore.

The boyfriend arrives.
Her make-up is askew.
Another little stroke?
He holds her hand,
silent.

The third week
she can't get off the toilet.
Her voice cracked, panicked –
'Nurse, Nurse!'

Relatives come from Tassie.
Whispered conferences in corridors.
His visits are briefer.

Fright in the whites
of her china eyes.
The dressing gown grows grubby.

The nurses struggle to dress her.

After six weeks, when I leave the ward,
she has stopped speaking. She lies there
waiting to be disposed of.

The Bed near the Window

'My son is a pilot' she says.
'He rang me yesterday
from America.'
She talks about him a lot.
Never about her daughter,
a nervous harried woman
who comes most days.

The son visits once.

She's well over eighty. Broke her leg
'pushing the Hoover into corners.'
From the street there's 15 steps
to her front door. 'But, no,
I'm not moving!'

Every day we exchange
encouragement, smiles.
But it doesn't do to talk much –
she doesn't like refugees, votes Liberal,
likes men more than women.
Idolises her dead father, dead husband.
The Son.

She reminds me of women of the Fifties
when I was growing up. Their innocence,
easy prejudice, wry bravery.

Women who served Kraft cheese
on Saos, slice of tomato,
a spring of parsley on top.

They had secret dreams –
if only to be a man.

Despite myself, I like her.
Sparky. Strong.
Despite herself, she is kind,
even, occasionally,
to her daughter

The Third Bed

She has the worst bed in the ward,
jammed against the only toilet.
So we lie closer together,
behind the curtains, she and I.

She is magnificent,
dark eyes black with suffering.
A hoarse whisper
produced with effort.

Showy flowers from friends
crowd her small space.
She is too sick to see visitors.

We hardly talk. No need.

She doesn't complain,
even when her handsome daughters
bicker across her inert body.
But her shame sears the thin
curtain between us.

In the evenings her husband
comes to brush her teeth.
He does it gently, taking care.

In that moment
I feel their contentment –
as if this is the best thing
he has ever done for her.

Suddenly she's worse.
Doctors, nurses, ward men,
wheel her in and out.

She endures, silent.
Yet behind the curtain
I almost touch her pain,
her fear.

Months later I see her in Outpatients.
We smile deeply into each others eyes.
Bonded in life, she and I.

The Fourth Bed

While in life simple sentences
elude me,
the novel in my head
flies along.

Each day provides a chapter —
a new visitor, a twist.
I lie absorbed, pretending
I'm not listening.

On the fourth bed
I lie stalled,
a long, long distance
from myself.

The terrifying future
ticks.

Going Home

Home, so familiar.
So strange.
Home hasn't changed.
I have.

Different selves –
one relieved
the other afraid.

Same landscape,
different universe.
How to find
new weapons?

Afterstroke

1.

What *is* the alphabet?
'a- b- c . . .'
Then nothing.

My stroke – own it –
blasted a hole in my brain.
Sounds, words, sentences
disappear like tumbleweed.

Numbers, modifiers,
prepositions
multi-syli-babble words –
once friends,
now baleful enemies.
Tiny connections making sense
of the world, and myself,
gone.

Hob-goblins prance and gabble
in the vacant space.

With a stroke of the pen
my writer's life erased.

2.

The pain comes later
It doesn't go away.

That's when, why,
I come undone.

3.

The goblins twist words
into skeins of gibberish.
A gaunt old woman drags
my right leg behind her

Inside a furious child,
red with rage,
fists gouging eyes,
trails after Mummy.
It hurts! Pick me up!

All potential mothers flee
in the face of this monster.

I don't write, save exercises:
Shopping Lists. Days of the Week.
Months of the Year. Post Code.
Vital Phone Numbers.
 I recite: 'B-P, P-B. B-P
Shoo-Coo, Coo-Shoo'
A fountain of self-pity
sprays ceaselessly.

Rupture

Inasmuch as anyone
knows anyone
I thought I knew you –
my love
partner
true friend.

Not this she-devil
spitting hate.
Murderous contempt
in your turning back.

I can't help
what I've become,
a ruined woman
turned ruinous.
Can't you see that?

Underneath this rubble,
it's still me calling.
Can't you hear that?

But maybe *I'm*
the spitting devil
furious beyond fury.
I see it in your
frightened
mirroring eyes.

Moving

I want to be a tortoise with
my house on my back.

This house, my beloved carapace,
has grafted itself onto my skin,
mixed with my bloodstream.

Sensible reasons to leave –
uneven ground, steep hills.
Necessary change.

But not now!
I need you, house,
to burrow down,
hide. Heal.

I need your delights
to soothe me.
The morning frosts,
small cobwebs lacing every fencepost
draping each bush in gossamer.
The way the sun settles to sleep
at the front gate each evening.

The first time I saw you
you fitted into my body.

It was the clump of late
winter daffodils that did it.

And the crooked turn in the corridor,
the ugly fire-place, the gun-cupboard
to turn into bookshelves.

Wintersweet outside the kitchen window.
Worn cast-iron in surprising places.
On the pond, the runic sundial,
slightly askew.

The mad jumble of your daily beauties.

I will leach you from my bones,
scrub you from my skin.
But take pity on me, beloved home.
Give me back a corner of my heart
so I can bear to leave you.

II

THE NEW HOUSE
POEMS

First Poem

An old garden seat,
a new bed of plants
flowering into the New Year.

Old fears, new fears.

Small shoots of thought
sustain me.
Help me, words –
you always have.

December 30, 2011

Looking Out

Thunder far off
               draws closer

The pines shiver
               grow dark

Everything waits
               the rain too

Drops hang loose
               in the air.

January, 2012

The Study

In my old home
it was a bit stately –
brown wood, bookcases
either side of
the unused fireplace.

A serious place
for the long haul.

In my new house
(not quite my home yet)
a small room, a long view
of tall pines.

A place for experiment –
dots, dashes, false starts,
riot effort sweat.

A study in bold –
red, yellow, black
with a dash of blue.

Bold colours to
hurl me into the future.

The Lounge Room

In the morning
light skitters from the fountain
onto the ceiling, falling gently
on furniture old and new.
My eyes rest on objects
in memory or affection.

In the evening
I sit in my new spot.
I can't change it now,
– how quickly habit forms –
 and watch the light fade.

In the old house the light
was dense in the tangled garden,
seeping in at windows –
so close!

Here it runs away
across an empty lawn
scoots the paddock
skims the glistening dam.

I watch like a cat, my eyes half-shut.

Lamp light now.
My father's lamp, the desk
my mother found in Boston.
In a silver frame, my sister,

aged three, in a Budapest park.
She twirls a little parasol.

Night is closing in.

The Library

It hardly deserves its name,
a tiny room snug
between our studies.

Books to the ceiling,
a daybed for dreaming,
a window looking to
long pines.

A dreamed-of space.
Even the least treasured book
schlepped from house to house –
talismans against a barbarous future.

The shelves are messy, random,
incomplete, much like a life.
Weighty classics still waiting,
faded Penguins, scribbled-over texts.
Small print I can't read any more.

An act of defiance, really,
building a library at all,
as books lie discarded
in junk shops and jumble sales.

An act of private faith, too,
putting our books together
after many years guarded
in separate rooms.

And Mirabile Dictu!
they fit as one.

Here are the signposts,
way-stations, of my sentient life.
From *Snuggelpot and Cuddlepie*
to *War and Peace* (still not read).
All witnesses, all present.

I would not mind dying here,
dreaming of the perfect book,
its bejewelled revelations,
its unerring truths holding me fast.

View from the Study

Hooped petticoats
in the foreground.
An old tree cascades
white blossoms.

In the home paddock
a day-old calf
teetering.

In the chook yard
five new eggs!

In the Gallery

1.

Many years ago
I saw a simple painting;
two ochre fields, one brown, one yellow,
a white line wandering
across the middle.

A shallow curve, I learned,
was an Aboriginal meeting place.
A knobbly swoop in the white line,
the site of a massacre.

I was caught forever.

Underneath the careful dotting
the rioting colours
I only catch a glimpse,
a glance – a slender bridge
to the other side.

In the new house we have built
a folly for these mysteries.
The front door opens on a long high room:
shimmering canvases from the deep desert,
the precise geometry of the Tiwi Islands,
bold works from Balgo, once a mission;
blues and greens from Bidyadanga
where red sand laps turquoise sea.

2.

Joan paints the life
of her father the stockman.
Angelina, nearing eighty,
inhabits her 'imagined country'
in much splendour.
They sing to each other across the room
But they keep their counsel, too

3.

I might meet an artist;
she might throw me a glance.
I'll praise the work, she'll smile a little.
Not much is said.

Yet somehow I feel them –
the old women sitting in the dust,
pulling pictures from their mind's eye.
The old men holding the law.

The myths and stories don't penetrate
my brain.
It's their paintings which beckon
and seduce.
Between bright paint and busy air
the ebb and flow of their spirits
are calling, pulling me in.

The Bedroom

In this space
where two embrace
no poems allowed!

In this room
dreams are private.
Poems have vanished.

In this space
of unadorned faces
all poems banished!

In this bedroom
poems that speak
with tongues and eyes

go unwritten.

The Wall of Women

In the new house, as in the old,
a wall brimming with portraits
of women.
They span a century, more.
Bold, shy, young, old,
known, obscure –
as are their painters.

At the centre is a serene painting
of the artist's wife, eyes cast down, reading.
A summer Sydney shimmers
at her elbow.

Others, their portraits like satellite moons,
gather around her as she sits absorbed:
My grandmother, in handsome young womanhood,
already on the stage of the Budapest Opera House.
Wendy Sharpe painting a woman in the nude,
and herself in the mirror opposite.
Both at their ease.
You can tell they are friends.

Below, a small nude, luminous
in creams blending to soft browns,
found in Rome. She, too, at ease.
The warmth between her and her painter,
sensual, without lust, warms my eyes.

Then gloomy, very English,
a Mrs Green. Her face a mask,
cardigan shrunk around her bony body.
Artist unknown.

Self-exiled in Paris,
Australian artist Bessie Davison,
aging and prim, caught
by a young Roy de Maistre.

I dream these women on my wall.
One day they will disperse again,
hang on other walls
in an endless re-arrangement
of time and space.

Others will dream their lives
differently, conjure other visions.
Somehow this unseen future
comforts me.

Butterfly Lane

While walking
down Butterfly Lane
in summer, a storm
of snowy butterflies
among straggly rows of ti-trees.

Nuggetty waxed flowers,
bees nuzzling their pinky hearts.
Two streams of ants in cross-file,
busy, busy.

The iridescent sap rising,
colours oozing blue-green
blood-red, honey-amber.

Since yesterday's rain
the roots sigh in relief.
Green twigs extend
their dainty points.

No need of distant stars
to remind me of my laughable
small self. Here at my shoulder,
another world – contiguous,
oblivious.

A gentle sky frames my view.
The earth spreads out below.

Annie

of the long legs and silver hair,
eyes of a sexy blue which challenge.

Annie: tough smart
kind no fuss fun.

Deeply complicated
but hides it well.

Annie of a thousand skills,
my busy bee

who could settle on fewer flowers
and drink more deeply of their content.

You have thirsty wells to fill
with pure cold water –

it's been a dry, parched year
leaving you bereft, sometimes brittle.

But (although you don't believe it)
you never break.

You have steel in your back,
the necessary splinter in your heart.

And I love the warmth and cold,
the steel and the fire.

The great withdrawal,
and the greater giving.

III

NIGHT

Michael

I see you,
hands to your head,
holding in the pain.
Reading a book
with fixed attention.
Plotting your intricate art –
the subtle perfection
in everything you did.

I see you
hands stabbing air
making a point – lots of points.
Holding a handkerchief
(always neat, always folded)
as you struggled to talk.

I never heard you
complaining.
Courageous, yes.
Often shitty too.
Garrulous, morose,
brilliant, learned,
loveable.

You held in your hands
– and in your lightning
blue-eyed gaze –

your contradictory,
mordant, ardent,
love-affair with life.

Martin. In Memoriam

Joie de vivre should have
been his middle name.
He gave chase to life,
gave it a run for its money.

Big in stature,
big in appetites, passions,
Big in dreams. Huge in
energy, generosity.

Eyes creased in mischief.
That absurdly cleft chin,
deep dimples, boom of voice.
The audacity and fun of him.

I loved serious Martin, too –
keen mind, quiet reading,
all curiosity and quickness.
The breadth and depth him.

Then Party Marty – fun fun fun!
Food, drink, ciggies,
more food, drink, ciggies
till dawn and beyond …

Then - often at the same time –
hard-working Martin,
exuberant talent and hard grind
balanced in equal measure

Lastly, gentle Martin
who loved his Adrian
– 'the old boy' –
with a steadfast heart.

His life cut short.
The misery and ache of it.
So many loved him,
none so more than

Susan
August, 2012

Enemy

Embedded in folds of skin
sunk deep in red tissue
imprinted in bones
my enemy lies.

Secret, silent, constant.

Diversion can trick it.
Only sleep defeats it.
By day I hold up words
like crosses – my holy weapons.

Poems my talismans.

I want to tame you
dark creature,
make use of you.
Come, eat from my hand.

I won't hurt you.

Just loosen your grip
and I'll find you a place
at my hearth
where we can both rest.

Come, pain.
Let's make truce.

Chatter

The Buddhists say
quiet the mind's chatter

Good task.
Hard ask.

Quiet the mind's chatter …

But what about
the babble and clatter
clutter and chaos
endless repetitions
repetitions …
The mad intrusions
crazed notions
inanity, dross
                    not to mention despair.

The sheer bloody boredom
of that cesspool called
The Mind.

Or more like a battered Red Rattler,
careening through ugly suburbs
past stations without stopping,
the PA turned up full volume
twenty-four-seven,
desperate people hanging
out the doors screaming –

all of them me.

But the Buddhists say
be patient.
Be in 'the moment'
whatever that brings.

The Buddhists say …

Turning 69

These last months I've been hovering
half-heartedly over a sketchy grave,
a foot, or just a toe, half in,
having a flirt and a feel.

How would it be?
Some mates already gone …
I'm very tired.
The pain gets to me.

But the dead don't want me yet.
They shovel me back towards
the living with worldly shrugs.

Shirker, they say.
So, it's getting harder?
So?
You haven't earned it yet –
The Big Sleep.

Jealousy

Little worm, nibbling
at the brain's edges,
sending its poisoned code
through the blood.

Jealousy retreats by day
dismissed by Reason;
creeps through the lines by night
to ambush defences at dawn light.

How cold, this jealousy.
It spreads its chill miasma,
imprisoning love
blotting out the sun.

Jealousy litters the field
with slain ideals.
It blunts actions,
murders affection.

Poisoned worm be gone!
Love and trust reign once more.
Let these gentle virtues
warm the bed we share.

Let our fingers join again.
May our eyes be search-lights
beaming light and love,
each to each. Each to each.

What is it?

I can't feel it.
It runs away.

No image comes to mind.
Just a distant smoke signal

on the edge of dreams.
I wake thinking nothing.

It's either before or after me.
A contortionist in my gut.

Nameless ills haunt me,
vanish, come again.

I can almost see it,
sidling around a corner.

Its name is almost on
my tongue.

It's called Fear.
That's what it's called.

Fear.

Stranger

She looks like someone I once knew
distorted in a fun parlour mirror.
The little bend in the back
now a gaping curve,
neat shoulders slung inwards.
Her avoiding eyes.

Sometimes I overtake her
on my walks.
I do know her, I think,
but there's a freezing
wind coming off her.
I can't get close.

If I make little overtures
my jokes fall flat.
Her voice comes from
far away. Out of tune.

When I get home
I avoid mirrors.

Just in case.

Crisis

If I lose my gift
– these scribblings on paper,
drowning signals
from atop high waves

What's left?

If I lose the greater gift
– or luck
of lasting love
given and received

What's left?

Only the tracery of trees,
a kernel of will,
and a faint whispering
of the heart

Listen. Wait.

IV

ALONE IN THE CITY

Sydney

It's been a long time,
you old harlot.
From my rented flat I see
your big-ticket items –
solid arc of Bridge,
a glinting sliver of Opera House.

Still heart stoppers, old girl.

This corner of The Cross is
the closest I'll get to Europe now.
You were my second home, Sydney,
until I deserted you for a quieter life.

Now I'm back, watching for clues, threads,
pushing my ailing body around your streets.

I take my small companion
onto your piss-riddled pavements
crazed with old tree roots.
She stops at every smell,
sniffs layer upon layer.

I sniff too – air heavy with
shops coffee noise food garbage –
and the heady scent of human stories.

In these back lanes
worn apartment buildings shrug off
druggies and drunks with weary elegance.
They whisper, 'come live amongst us,
we'll weave you close again'.

Sydney you old harlot,
press your brittle bones against
my warming skin.
Make me feel alive again.

Morning in The Cross

March. The longest month.
Sydney sweats.
Buildings smell of unwashed bodies.
Sulo bins sprawl across pavements,
mouths agape.

Down a back lane, two old men.
One leans from his ground-floor window,
the other stands on the footpath.
They exchange a plastic bag.
Money? Food? Drugs?
A video?

I sit in Fitzroy Gardens,
the Fountain at my back.
A shabby dog ambles by.
Sarah sparkles, play-bows, wags.
But he sniffs, sighs, moves on.
'He's old,' says his owner.
We raise rueful eyebrows.
She looks past her best, too,
as do I.

Across the road, the Croissant d'Or.
It's been around since croissants
were a novelty. Warm pastry fills
my nostrils. Ten dollars
in my pocket...

Down the street the tiny bookshop,
Clays, is closing after 60 years.
Last week the sad-eyed man at the counter
said the business was 'in negotiations'.
Today it's in darkness, shelves bare,
books banished.

Local readers are in mourning.

The Thai is offering $10 lunches.
I begin to worry about it too…

I see a famous face – if you watch SBS –
emerge from the florist. She's been
reading news for a long time.
A survivor!

Almost at my door
Sarah finally squats. I clean it up.
A street sweeper with an old-fashioned
broom smiles at me. I smile back.
He points towards his bin.

Here, There

Here, a small flat
shaded by one generous tree.
A brochure-blue pool.

There, a big house,
garden, stables, paddocks.
Long horizons.

Here, traffic bellows.
Streets heave, sirens shriek.
Trucks racket and spew.

There, magpies, currawongs.
The tin roof pings and pops
as it cools.

Here, a zigzag of tall towers.
Hardy plants battle bitumen.
A tangle of bodies, buildings.

There, earth and sky. Seasons.
Wattle fading, ti-tree coming on.
Two people lost in a flawed paradise.

I feel lonely in that quiet county,
often content in this city's furore.
I track between two places

here, there,
everywhere, nowhere,
               putting up small flares.

Sarah's Dilemma

The smells at every tree, post,
corner, the pats of passers by.
Everything new, everything exciting!

But to get to the big street,
the lead, the silly poo bag,
Mum's handbag swinging
wildly above my head.
The lift, its noise and lights,
doors moving in and out!

The horrible heavy front door.

Once we're in the street,
Mum pushes and pulls half-
way through the best smells,
ties me to a rail and disappears.
'Be good, Sarah, good Sog'.
And then she's gone.

Oh tremble!
Tremble!

On the way home I stay close.
The lift again, the huge door …
Inside. Lead off.
Cuddles. My bed.

I have her all to myself.
I'm beginning to like it here.

Now we are moving again.
Back to the farm.

Joy!
Other Mother,
Ginger, Bodhi,
their safe smells.
Trees, cows, horses.
No lead.
I can run!

But they're packing the car …
What if Mum goes off without me?
Tremble!

She lifts me in.

Haiku

1

Last days of autumn.
Greedy eyes grab
fistfuls of colour
for winter.

2

Down Down Down
Rain in sheets pours
drips. Rain on rooves
pounding the black night.

3

Like a dog dozing
waiting for night to
swallow the hours.
Survival.

Early Morning

Rain has fallen.
A little cooler today.
People stride with purpose.
Women in big boots, spiky heels.
Men in the latest imported sneakers.

Too early for beggars.

Take-away coffees are de rigueur.
People stand waiting for as long
as it would take to sit.
They look at the ground,
search their mobiles.
No one talks.

Autumn leaves
smear the footpath.

Nurse Jenny of Prunes

Who is this officious creature?
Bustling, busy, loud.
You can't miss her.
Can't stand her.

Third miserable morning.
The broken wrist hurts.

For the second time, no breakfast.
And no life-saving PRUNES!
I see red. I yell, I rant.
Then I cry.

'Get me some PRUNES,'
she barks down the phone,
'It's more than my life's worth!'

'It's not about breakfast,' I whimper.
She shrugs, rolls her eyes …
No sympathy there.

Stand off. I watch, listen.
She's the best nurse on the floor.
Kind, funny, knows her stuff.

Overtures on both sides.
We start to laugh.
Keep laughing.

How quickly dislike turns
into a kind of love.

V

BRUNSWICK HEADS

Spring in Brunswick Heads, 2013

To Julia Gillard

1.

Delicate ears of coastal grevilleas dance,
lemon, gold, cream, every kind of red,
tiny antennae curled into the breeze.

Crimson bougainvillea across the lane
lunges towards our veranda.
The sturdy palms, once slender saplings,
sport age-rings around their middle.
Arcs of red seeds hang from their belts.

Holiday time.
Kids swarm about the town.
Swimming, ice cream and bikes
fill their days.
Life's nasty surprises have not
exploded at their feet yet.

Last night on the telly,
I saw Julia for the first time
since The Fall.
Her eyes alive again.
Her charm, having deserted her
in high office, is back.

The exploding hand-grenades of hatred
may have singed her skin
but did not scar her soul.

There's still a young girl in there,
remembering ice cream, bikes,
and dreams of changing the future.

This morning, a lone pelican on the river.
Ungainly, stately, silly, wise.

What greater miracle
than a pelican?
I wish Julia long life
and a pelican each day.

Birds of a Colour

On the placid river pelicans
laze in elegant morning suits
of black and white.
Their pink beaks and gobs
a playful inspiration
of the Colour God

Late afternoon.
Pauper-grey swifts
agile overhead.
As they wheel close
a warmth of brown,
a surprise of blue.
Their backdrop grey
now precise,
just right.

A frenzy of dusk parakeets.
Their uproar and the failing light
confound their fabled colours.
But just above, a clutch
of birds in deep-green coats,
and in the higher branches,
a multitude in vivid Joseph cloaks.

A last flamboyant visitation
from the Colour God.

Black Waves

Safe on the familiar shore, I watch you.
You paddle toward the waves, unthinking.

Your arms lengthen, legs in rhythm
as a hazy horizon disappears.

In an instant black waves rear.
Steep curling killers.

Your limbs constrict, head tosses.
Undertow buckles your belly.

The black waters swirl, break up,
leaving you gasping, empty.

Grit in every fold of skin.
Muck in every pore.

I call and call.
But you won't come in.

2.

Uneasy calm.
            Sun shines on water.
                        A gull dips.

Your body floats, arms out
       Warm currents
              gentle you.

Then a small rumble.
       Louder. Louder.
              Your ears don't hear.

On the nearing horizon
       the steep waves rebuild,
              Your eyes don't see.

The waves rush, rush away
       spitting angry sand.
              Again. Again.

You half-turn to the familiar shore.
Then you swim out, mesmerised,
              to the brawling sea.

    3.

Long hours after, I leave the beach.
You skulk in my shadow, sullen.

At home in a quiet room
I argue with you, blind fool –
what compulsion sends you
to the repeating waves

like a gambler back to the machine
or lovers back to the smouldering rope
that burns them?

Stop this mad drum beat.
Don't stop your ears.
Don't shut your eyes.

But you're deaf to entreaty
my demon swimmer.
In the quiet room I stare
into your fevered eyes

4.

For months at a time, demon,
I evade you, like a crab scuttling
sideways before the oncoming tide.
Then you flare – white steel,
summer lightning.
My hiding-places smashed,
washed away.

Yet if lose my fear,
if I can lance your malice,
you might give up your power.
Then gently, tentatively, we might
make peace.

For Annie on her 58th Birthday

Providence wings you
all the way from China
for both our birthdays.
A quarter of a century

marked in little rituals.
which never weary us.

We've been through conflagrations:
brush fires, long-lasting flames,
downright infernos, unhappy embers.
Some blazes still to come.

We survive with love and courage,
my life's dear companion.

It takes a lot, this being together –
subtlety, persistence, patience,
seizing moments of joy.
Somehow we fit, my Annie.

I never understood love until
the gods gave me the gift of you.

Dogs

You outlive them
over and over.
Each dog woven
into your being.
Each death scars the heart.

This time it's Ginger,
big golden girl,
gentle, stubborn,
back legs going.

Dogs have no gap, as we do,
between their bodies and themselves.
If bored they sleep.
Unhappy, they won't eat.

We watch over Ginger,
weigh the options,
casting for a little bridge
across the chasm of language.

She whimpers, sighs,
struggles to get up.
Her eyes speak pain
yet her inner light is steady.

The gifts she has given us.
The love we give her back.

When she's ready
will she give us a sign?

VI

RAFT

b

Refuge

1.

Forty years ago, we slept on the floor
of a small fibro house scrounged
from the Housing Commission.
We called it Bonnie's
and waited
for the first desperate women
to fall in the door, trailing kids.

A cup of tea.
A life story.

In the morning the kids played
in the dusty back yard, safe –
for now.

People gave blankets, sheets, chairs.
Because this place of shelter
was needed.

Forty years later
Bonnie's is still here.
A bigger better house.
Other houses. Offices!
Paid staff.

This sole survivor
of the refuge movement
is still needed.

In dark truth
needed more,
as men, pickled
in resentment,
brined in hatred,
continue to kill.

2.

Today a 40th birthday bash
for Bonnie's
Yellow balloons in the courtyard.
Yellow and black posters everywhere
saying 'You are NOT powerless.'

Swings and slides for the kids.
A row of suited men,
respectfully silent
in a sea of elated women,

On leaflets, brochures, lips,
an old phrase to gladden my heart –

'By Women, For Women'

3.

1975.
International Women's Year
Whitlam's comet in brief trajectory

A Government was listening!

We were young, or youngish.
We marched in the streets one day,
wrote submissions the next.
Hoped for funding,
found a house and opened
anyway.

What really mattered then
– or now –
Words or Actions?

I always thought words.
They enshrine action,
pinning the butterfly
to the page, trapping action
beyond its brief life.

But looking back
across oceans of words,
expended, written, read,
I wonder.

Is it Action,
its simplicity, courage,
rush and surge
which truly transforms?

Not books in their stillness,
shut fast upon shelves.

And yet … a phrase,
a half-forgotten conversation,
a potent submission,
can be subterranean weapons,
torpedoes, depth charges
erupting into action,
here, now!

We descend to the street
brandishing placards in bold –

> **'You are
> NOT
> powerless'**

In Time

In time, memories
of war become tame,
fading battle scars.

With time, battlefields
become fields of crosses,
become fields of flowers,
become crops.

In time, a familiar
compulsion takes root,
blooms, a vast black poppy
pollinating across continents
and oceans.

In no time,
men gather in their millions,
They fight. They die,
plunging deep to a seabed
stacked with their own bones.

Raft

One by one we gather on this haphazard craft.
We touch finger tips, speak in gentle code.
Old friends, glad of each other's warmth.

Long or short?
It's anyone's guess,
this voyage out.

The raft drifts.
We watch the horizon
hoping for a multi-coloured dusk,
dreading violent storms.

The raft holds,
lashed together by old ties.

Mother in the Land of Dreams

You almost disappeared
even from the land of dreams.
A few shadowed appearances,
the odd cameo role.

Once you were lying
on a red floor
in our old eat-in kitchen
with my sister.
I wasn't frightened,
just pleased to see you.

Then you faded to black.

How I missed you then.

Some twelve years later
you're back! Full-length
technicolour epics.
Always in the right,
always irritating.
Loved.

Other people appear
morph, meld, disappear,
in the way of dreams.
But you are whole, real.

I knew you wouldn't die
while I was alive
to dream you.

Contentment

For Robert Dessaix

'Contentment,' my old friend said.
'Not a word favoured by the young …
'Yes, I think I'm content.'

His words came back to me
as I went for a piss in the night.
(Old woman's bladder,
another friend calls it.)

Contentment – a word
to savour, roll on the tongue.
But it's not for me, is it?
A ridiculous idea …
however delightful.

Yet something similar steals
over me like a warming coat
and promises to stay awhile.

A slippery word,
contentment.
As slippery as a mirage
on a narrowing horizon.

As slippery as trying
to catch and land
a good poem.

Acknowledgements

I have always thought of myself as a prose writer. But on the eve of 2012, I took a new path for various reasons, many of which you will have gathered by now.

I had written some poetry previously, but rarely for publication. This time, as poetry took over completely, I was on a steep learning curve and I relied a lot on my friends and other writers as sounding boards and mentors. Over the years many got a poem or two on email. To mention everyone would make for an embarrassingly long list, but I thank you all for encouragement and insights.

Other people I pestered with more poems and for more detailed feedback. And all gave me penetrating comments and much to think about. My thanks to: Helen McCue, Jan Kenny, Elizabeth Taylor, Valerie Hardy, Lyn Clarke, CJ Juby, Jean-Christophe Burckhardt, Meryl Constance and Lucy Bainger.

A bow of gratitude to Kerry Willis, my old schoolmate. At a time of great loss for Kerry, I tentatively sent her a poem. She told me later she had pinned it on the wall and read it every morning. Whenever I got discouraged and thought 'this is all crap', I thought of her.

I'm also grateful to Julianne Schultz and her 'poetry adviser' for publishing 'Sydney', unsolicited, in the incomparable *Griffith Review*. That gave me a real boost.

To artist and friend Dale Dean for her constant encouragement and feedback, and for allowing her remarkable painting to be reproduced on the cover of *Rupture*. Also for her inventive and lovely artworks, inspired riffs on the poetry.

Many of my writer friends gave me their patient scrutiny. My deepest thanks to:

Jen Reidy, who shared her fine poetry with me and helped me with mine.

Judy Langton, my sister, also a fine poet, for her generosity in letting me onto her patch, and her acute eye.

My (currently hibernating) writing group in the Southern Highlands for encouraging reactions to early poems.

In the Northern Rivers, to Bev Sweeny and Jane Camens for giving me such good feedback.

Thank to you to Emma Ashmere, for her discerning taste and unstinting support.

Robert Dessaix, treasured friend and down-to-earth adviser.

To Sarah Day for kindly reading some poems and giving me the benefit of her considerable expertise.

Suniti Namjoshi, admired poet and good friend for her subtle guidance.

And to Jared Gulian, for his keen intelligence and his and CJ's support throughout.

Two special people stand out and deserve my love and thanks. Andrea Goldsmith who put her novelist's instincts and deep knowledge of poetry into many drafts. And Lesley Lebkowicz, whose poetry I much admire and who has been a constant mentor over several years.

A huge salute to Terri-ann White, a beacon in the troubled world of publishing and the best publisher a writer could have.

Finally, to my fellow writer, partner, and dear love, Anne Coombs; the patient reader of too many drafts and, as always, my final arbiter. Thank you for living with me through the painful and rewarding years of writing *Rupture*.